Chris Brazel

Samuel James Edward Fox

How Dad and I Became Mates

Chris Brazel, Author

The moral rights of the Author have been asserted in accordance with the Copyright, Design and Patents Act, 1988.

All rights reserved. No part of this publication may be reproduced, stored in retrieval system or transmitted in any form or by any means, electronic, mechanical, photocopying, recording or otherwise without the prior permission of the Publisher.

The information in this book is the author's opinion and experiences. You must form your own opinion and make your own choices. You need to consider the appropriateness of the information in this book in relation to your own personal circumstances. If you have a medical condition, you must first consult with your doctor.

Chris Brazel Enterprises Pty Ltd (Publisher) Chris Brazel, Author or the editor shall not be liable (including liability for negligence) for any loss or damage arising out of the information or your use of this book.

First published in 2022 by Chris Brazel Enterprises Pty Ltd, 5/43 Upper Brookfield Rd., Brookfield. QLD. 4069.

ISBN 978-0-9805800-8-2

Special thanks to:
Editor & Proof Reading – Marcelle Charles, Koa Park & Mila Park
Cover, Design & Graphics – Chris Brazel & Mindy Gilling

Contact the Author by email at chris@chrisbrazel.com.au.
If you would like to know more about Chris Brazel's work or order books check out her website www.chrisbrazel.com.au

Please enjoy the book, as much as Chris Brazel had writing it.

This book is dedicated to all dads who take the time
to know their sons and daughters.

Chris Brazel

Chapters

1. Another School
2. Nan and I come up with a Plan
3. Meeting Henry C
4. New School Day 2
5. Action Plan for the New Body
6. Things Come Crashing Down
7. The Championships
8. We Found a Way to Love and to be Mates

Another School

It's Friday afternoon and my last day at this school.

I hope Mum is picking me up and not Dad. I know he is going to be furious with me. My ears are going to be hurting like mad, along with my head.

I just don't know why I cause them so many problems. I don't mean to. It just seems to happen.

I wish the Principal would have seen and heard what the other boy was doing and saying to me. Everyone always only sees me as the problem. They never stop to listen to my side of the story. They jump to conclusions that because I have been in trouble before and accused of causing problems, they think I am the problem again.

No wonder I am getting fatter and fatter. I just want to eat my life away. Who cares really what I look like. Nobody seems to worry about my feelings.

The kids at school tease me. My Dad is always going off about the way I look and calling me fat and lazy. My Mum just sits back and allows it all to happen.

I wish my Nan was here. At least I know she loves me. I could sure do with one of her amazing hugs at the moment. She always makes sure that you know everything is going to be ok. She sees life differently to everyone else through her rosy, red glasses.

While I have been waiting for one of my parents to pick me up, I looked up to the sky to make sure that no tears were allowed to come. Next minute this magpie flies past and does a poo right onto my jumper. Now I am going to be in even bigger trouble. I can just hear it now – "How could you ruin your school jumper?" There will be no questions of, "How did you get your jumper like that?" There will be no checking to see if I am ok and if the magpie hurt me or swooped at me. Oh no, it will be immediately my fault, and I caused it.

Really when you think of it, how stupid it is to think that I made a magpie poo on me.

Well, that is my life and how everyone immediately jumps to conclusions that I cause my own problems.

Oh no, I see a car turning into the school driveway and it looks like it's Dad. Well in some way I may as well get the ear twist and knock over the head sooner rather than later. I know it is going to happen, at least getting it sooner, by the time we get home he will be ready to tell me he loves me, give me a pretend hug and say that he will stand by me.

So hard to know. Does my Dad love me or hate me?

One minutes I am in big trouble, getting my ear twisted and a slap over the head and the next he is giving me a hug with lots of empty words.

I opened the car door and sure enough, the slap over the head came first, then his words, "Samuel James what are we going to do with you? How many schools do we have to send you to? Your mother and I are beside ourselves knowing what goes on in your head to be always causing these problems."

"But Dad I didn't really do anything. This kid was teasing me about my weight, and he tried to trip me so as I was falling, I brushed him, and he fell over. If he had not tried to trip me, then I would not have brushed him as I was falling. The other kids saw it, but they stuck up for the other kid and would not tell the truth. He kept calling me names all day about being fat."

"Well, Samuel James, you are in fact carrying too much weight. You need to get off all the junk food and start trimming down. We both know that.

You will be off to a new school next week. It will be interesting to see how long you last there."

Those were his last words. His mobile rang, thank heavens and he was back into his work, nice and polite as usual.

We arrived home and sure enough Mum was in the same mood. At least she did not grab my ear. She decided I could just go to my room, with no afternoon tea and was politely informed that there would be no dinner either to see if missing out on meals might help me to wake up to myself.

I just headed to my room and closed the door. Little did they know I had a stash of food in a box in my cupboard. I have got used to this treatment so now I just plan ahead.

They can't say I am that dumb if I can at least look after myself this way.

I sat on the bed and started to snack on this huge block of chocolate. I then pulled out my Nan's picture and looked at it and made a wish that she would come and visit soon.

She is amazing and very much in touch with life. Whenever I hold her picture and really, really focus on the fact that I need her, she always rings or just turns up. She taught me on one of her visits about mind messages and how when you love someone you can always feel and sense their messages when they come from the heart.

I put the chocolate bar down and held her picture next to my heart and I just focused on my mind message to her. I sent her these messages that I needed her to rescue me or if she could not rescue me at least come and visit and give me one of her amazing hugs.

I kept focusing on my messages. I was totally determined to make sure that my mind message would get through.

I then decided that eating the chocolate bar was not really going to do me any good. Maybe I am the one at fault. Maybe I am useless and worthless.

I mean when I look in the mirror, I do look a little fat. Maybe Dad is right, and I will never make anything of myself.

As all these thoughts were going over in my head, I ended up falling asleep.

It was the weekend. Dad was away playing golf with his mates. Mum decided that while Dad was away, she would have the girls over for a few glasses of wine and a chat about life.

It was decided that as I was still in trouble, I would spend my time in my room as my punishment for having to go yet to another school.

Just before Mum's friends arrived, my prayers were answered, and Nan was on the phone asking to chat with me. WOW, it always works. She loves me so much she can always tell when I really need her.

Mum handed the phone over and I suggested to Mum that I take it into my room so as not to disturb her while she was getting ready for her friends. She agreed, so I headed to my room for a one-on-one private conversation with Nan.

Nan will know what to do. She always has a way to find solutions to any problem that there is.

You never know when Nan and I put our heads together magic just starts to happen.

She always says, where there is a will there is always a way.

Samuel James Edward Fox

Nan and I come up with a Plan

I quickly closed the door behind me and headed to my bed where I could chat and look out the window at the same time.

"Hi Nan, how are you?"

"Great, my lad, but I have a feeling you are not so great. I got a few mind messages last night and they seemed rather sad. Tell me what is happening in your world?"

"Well, it is like this Nan. I got expelled from school and have to go to another school. Dad said he is not going to waste any more money on private schools for me anymore. I have to go to a public school, as he thinks I am just a waste of time and money."

"Oh, dear me! Looks like we better sort out a plan for a solution or two," Nan replied.

I said, "Oh, Nan, can I just come and live with you? That would be the best solution."

"I don't think your parents are going to agree to that, so let's look at other solutions," Nan replied. I agreed.

Nan then asked when I would be starting at the new school. I said, "Monday." She then replied, "Well, we better think fast.

Ok, let's see how we start to train your brain to start to attract different energies to you. It seems to me that you just keep attracting the wrong energy. We are going to have to change that.

I need you to take a look around your room. I have been reading a few books written by Chris Brazel who is achieving amazing things with children. She says that you always start with your brain codes, so you know how your mind works, then you work on your bedroom, then you work on words and exercises.

Are you ready to see if we can fix this, my lad?"

"Yes, Nan, I am so ready to fix my problems. I don't think my ears can keep going at this rate. They are surely going to change shape."

"Ok, my lad, now let's look at your brain codes and see if we can work them out. I bought Chris Brazel's books and one of them is called 'Me and My Codes.'

First, we need to look at your natural code as that is what you do naturally. It is also what you need in your life naturally. It is like you can't go without this energy.

Ok, seeing as you are born on the 28th that means you are always in transition. You are moving from one thing to another. So as soon as you get somewhere, you don't stay long then you are onto the next thing."

"Ah, Nan, that would be right. I no sooner get to a new school, than I am off to the next school. How do we fix that?"

"Well hang on let's go through all the codes.

The year you were born is the next one which is your path code and that comes to 18/9. 18/9 means that you are torn between the material and the spiritual. You need to finish things off, but often don't. Also, it is important that you do not have too many processed foods as they can make you put on weight," she replied.

"Well, Nan, you are right again. I don't finish things off, I certainly eat lots of processed foods and I guess you could say they are the main reason why I am fat. How many brain codes does a boy have?"

"Well, you have 8 brain codes, but we are going to work on 4. I think that will be enough.

The next one is your unblocking code and that is an 8. That means you are an achiever. Life is karmic. You can get lots of help from above and by that, I mean the universe, or some people may say God or angels."

"Well, that sounds great Nan, but I really don't think I have achieved very much in my life or that I am going to achieve much in life at the rate I am travelling at the moment."

"Never you mind, young man, are you forgetting that I am by your side and what do I always tell you? I tell you where there is a will there is always a way. Now let's look at the last code and that is your lucky code which is 1, so that means when we work on what helps you to create luck in your life, we are helping you do what is natural for you. You see the 28 reduces to 10 then 1. We can sort this out. I know we can.

Do you know how you love to look through the windows? Well, the reason you love looking out your windows is that they connect to your number 1 brain code. When you look through a window you see different things to what is in the room you are in. It is like you get to see another story.

The best thing about your 1 code is that you have it twice, so we are kind of fixing two problems at once.

With the 1 code, your bedroom is very important, so do you reckon we have time now to work on your room? What is your Mum doing now?" Nan asked.

"Hang on Nan, let me go and check." I raced out to the kitchen and sure enough Mum was there with her friends who had started to arrive. I went back into my room and said to Nan, "We will be fine. Mum is busy with her friends."

"Ok, young man, let us get started, was Nan's reply.

Step One.

Stand at the door and look into your room. What do you see first of all?"

"Well, when I stand at the door and look in, I have my shoes lying on the floor along with my clothes from yesterday. Then I have a hook on the wall where I was going to put a picture. I have my desk which is rather messy and my bed which I have not made. What does that say about me?"

"Lots young man. With your 9 code it is about finishing things so when you see your messy bed that means you are telling yourself that you never finish things and things are a mess. What is the design of your quilt?"

"Well, I don't like it much, as it has all these circles that just go into each other. It makes my mind dizzy. I did tell Mum, but she decided she liked it, and it was going to stay."

"I know what we can do. How about I buy you a new quilt then your Mum can't say anything as she will not want to offend me."

"That is a great plan, Nan. Thank you."

"Next, I want you to go to your bed and see if you feel it is in the control position."

"What do you mean by that, Nan?"

"Well, stand at your bed and see if you can see the door and the window and if you feel positive and confident."

I walked over to my bed, and found that it was in the control position as I could see both the door and the window. One tick on the boxes.

"Ok, that is great. I will look at buying you a new quilt. What I need for you to do is make sure you make your bed each morning. Can you tidy up your shoes and put them in the closet and tidy up your clothes? When you take your clothes off, if they are dirty, you put them into the laundry basket and if they are clean, you put them away."

"Yes, Nan, I can do that."

"Great my lad," Nan replied.

"Now for the hook on the wall. Do you have a picture that we can put on that hook," Nan asked.

"No, sorry Nan, I don't."

"That is ok, son, how about along with the quilt I buy a picture that goes on the wall. I will get one of Chris Brazel's prints. She has a great selection and we can match that with the quilt. What do you think?" Nan asked.

"Great, is there anything else we need to do?" I asked.

"No," Nan replied.

You know what I was starting to feel better already. I had my Nan by my side.

I said goodbye and Nan agreed to check on me again the following day. We had a plan. I had someone who cared and loved me by my side.

I tided up my room, put my shoes away, put all my clothes away and climbed into bed. I must say I actually felt ok. I also didn't need to go to my stash and get chocolate. I was full but with love instead of chocolate.

The morning came and I was up early. I made my bed like my Nan had asked and went out to see my Mum. Dad was still away with his golfing mates.

Mum then said that my Nan had already called and said she had a present for me and was coming over. I already knew what the present was, so I had a little chuckle to myself.

Mum walked passed my room and saw the bed made and how tidy it was. She turned to me and said, "What is going on? You never make your bed or tidy your room?"

I just replied that I thought that seeing I was going to a new school, I should start to try and change my life and I was going to start with my room.

Mum just nodded her head and said, "Well, let us see how long this lasts."

Little does my Mum know that I am on the road to changes in my life. I know that she is going to be proud of me and the changes. Even, more importantly, I am going to be proud of me.

Nan arrived later in the afternoon. Lucky Mum wanted to go out so asked if Nan could stay with me until she got back. Our plan of action was working. I bet Nan had made a wish to have Mum go shopping so we could have time alone.

Nan handed me my two large parcels. One was my quilt which I knew was coming. I opened the wrapping and there it was. It looked happy and powerful at the same time. One side was navy with tiny lines of red and white stripes. They were very thin. The other side was just white. The pillowcases were navy with white piping and little shields in the centre.

I then opened my other parcel, and it was a picture of a horse standing next to a boy and looking at sheep in a paddock.

It matched my quilt.

We quickly changed the quilt and the pillowcases. We then placed the framed print on the wall.

You could feel the most amazing energy in my room. It was like it belonged to someone. That someone was me.
I must say I felt like a king with power to speak and rule over my life.

I gave Nan the biggest hug ever. Then, just when I thought I had all my gifts, she pulled out another small parcel and said this is a really special one, open it and see.

I said thank you and opened the parcel. Inside was a set of rubber balls. There were red, orange, green and navy blue balls. Each ball had written the words MINDFIT Champions. They looked awesome.

I turned to Nan and said, "What do you do with them?"

Nan replied, "They are part of a Creative Brain Training Programme where Chris Brazel teaches children to train their brain to be confident, positive and powerful. You can also train for her special MINDFIT Championships which are held each year in QLD.

I made an appointment to speak with Chris Brazel and told her a few things, not that you have to tell her anything. Once she knows your date of birth, she does the codes and gives you a plan to win in life.

Because of your 2 x 1 codes working with a ball in sport will be the ultimate way to help you train your brain to what you want. I can show you how to kick off with the ball games, then you will be able to practise each day. Each colour has a different energy and different ways it will connect to your mind.

When you want to be super powerful and confident, you will work with the red ball. When you want to feel happy and find answers, you will work with the yellow ball.

When you want to connect to your heart and feel love and peace, work with the green and when you really want to connect to your soul and inner guidance and knowledge, you will work with the navy blue. What do you think? Shall we give it a go?"

Tears came to my eyes. What would I do without my Nan? She always has the solutions to help me get through life.

I must say I loved her next comment which was, "Did you know you have a couple of codes similar to Tiger Woods? Chris Brazel said that golf would be a great way for you to work with your brain codes and become the most amazing sportsperson and the achiever you want to be."

I gave Nan the biggest hug I could give. She gave me a kiss on the cheek and said, "Let's go outside while your Mum is away and start training that brain of yours to be confident, powerful, resilient and, most of all, the achiever you were born to be."

We headed outside to an area where we could bounce the ball on the ground and then against the wall.

Nan suggested that we start with the red ball at first to build confidence and to get a goal and a focus.

She taught me two exercises to work with and the words to go with those two exercises.

The first one was that you bounce the ball to the ground and work with both hands saying as you bounce the ball, "Whatever happened yesterday is all gone now." Once you do 9 times with those words and two hands together, you then just work with the right hand, then the left hand then right, left, right.

As soon as I started to bounce the ball, it felt like I was moving into control, and I had this amazing feeling of freedom and confidence all at the same time. Nan was bouncing her ball with me. She had brought an extra set so that she could work with the exercises with me.

Once we did all the sections to the floor the next move was to toss to the wall. When you toss to the wall that is when you are training your brain that you are breaking through to what you want. You change the words, and you go back to working with both hands at first, 9 times, then you only use your right hand, then your left hand and then right, left, right.

The words apparently are the power of brain training. The words for me to use were, "I am doing great at my new school, I have friends and I am achieving great things."

It was interesting when I was tossing the ball with my right hand it was easy, but when I went to my left hand, I started to miss the ball. Nan said that it was ok and that it was just my brain connecting to the messages that I was trying to give it.

Nan worked beside me with her ball, it was so much fun.

After we did all the sections, we moved to the last one which was my favourite. You toss the ball to the sky, then catch it and start all over again.

We both went through the exercises about 10 times. It was lIke neither of us wanted to stop or give up. It was fun, it was powerful and best of all I felt amazing. I was also working up a sweat, so the exercise was going to help me with my weight.

All of a sudden I heard the front door and it was Mum back home again.

Nan went inside to say hello and showed her my new quilt and picture in my room. That was going to save me trying to explain.

Mum was ok with the changes. Well, she never said anything to my Nan, I guess she was not game to say anything. Nan is rather powerful in her own way.

Soon it was time and Nan had to head off home. I gave her another huge hug and a big thank you.

We had a little wink to each other which is our secret way of acknowledging that we have a plan.

I went outside to the backyard and got back into my exercises. It was like my brain knew that this was needed if I was ever going to make it in the world.

I had a big day ahead of me tomorrow and I wanted to be as powerful, confident and in a good head space as much as I could.

I decided to put my red ball into my school bag so when I got to school and if I was having a bad time, I could work with my ball just like Nan said.

This lad was going to be ok. I could just feel it in my bones.

Samuel James Edward Fox

Meeting Henry C

Meeting Henry C

Mum decided she would be the one to drop me off to my new school.

We arrived and Mum and I headed to the Principal's office. We were able to go straight in and meet her. She seemed really nice. She welcomed me to my new school and said that if I had any problems her door was always open, and I could come and see her.

I said, "Thank you."

Mum left and I was shown by the Principal's assistant where my classroom was. I must admit I was feeling a little nervous but strangely, since working with the ball and having it in my school bag, I felt like I would be ok. Since bouncing with the ball, it is hard to explain but, once you get into the exercises, it is like your worries all go and you feel confident and powerful all at the same time.

I went into my classroom and met my teacher. She also seemed lovely. Was this school going to be different from the rest? Maybe public schools are the way to go. The kids in my classroom all seemed to be friendly. Nobody was actually making faces at me. When we went to lunch, even though I didn't have any friends, at least none of the boys were teasing me about being fat.

I found a quiet area behind the classrooms where there was cement to bounce my ball on and a wall to toss to. I was on a mission to keep my mind in the right place.

I kicked off with the ball to the ground. Next I started to toss to the wall when this kid with crazy red hair and large white glasses came up to say hello. He looked rather short and young, so I knew he was in a lower grade than me.

He bowled up and said, "Hello, I am Henry C. Welcome to our school. What is your name?"

I was a little thrown back by his confidence and power in his voice. I replied, "My name is Samuel James Edward Fox, Samuel James for short."

He just looked at me and said, "WOW. That is a name and a half. It is worse than Merthyr Thomas Waterhouse."

I said, "What do you mean?" He then replied, "Oh it is just a friend of mine at the school, who is an awesome person but when she started at the school, she was being bullied but then I showed her how to work out her brain codes and how to find her confidence. That is what I do around here you know."

I looked at him then said, "Would that be the brain codes that Chris Brazel has developed which are so amazing?" He then replied, "Yes, have you had your codes done?" I then said, "Yes, my Nan got them for me to help me as I was not having such a great time with being bullied and the last school I got expelled from. Besides my Dad and I kind of don't get along. He thinks I am a waste of space and money."

Henry C then looked me right in the eye and said, "Listen here SJ. Nobody is a waste of time and money and certainly not you. Let's get this ball rolling by shortening that name to SJ. Why carry all that weight with all those names? What do you think?"

I looked at him and immediately said, "WOW that is awesome, I feel so much lighter already. It was like I was carrying all this weight."

"Great, my man. Now tell me, did your Nan also sign you up to the CB Club which Chris Brazel has for children, young people and adults?" Henry C replied.

I said, "I am not sure, but I can find out if you like." Just then the bell went, and it was time to go back into school. We agreed to meet the following day and Henry C was going to invite Merthyr T to come and join in as well.

It felt awesome. First day at this new school and I already had a friend. Not a pretend friend but a friend who was interested in me.

Mum picked me up and it was nice to see she had a smile on her face. Maybe things were changing in all directions.

We got home and I headed immediately to do my homework. I was totally going to take responsibility for my actions and myself at this new school.

As I was working on my homework, I heard music in the kitchen. I walked out and sure enough Mum was really pumping with the music. She was cooking a new recipe for dinner. She always looks so beautiful when she is happy. It is like my Mum is two different. A sad one who looks lost and a happy one who looks beautiful.

It was not long, and Dad was home. He also had a great day. We all had dinner, the new recipe was awesome. I volunteered to do the dishes. Both Mum and Dad looked at me with a smile. Dad then said, "This new school could be just what you need." I agreed.

I headed off to my room and finished off my homework. I was ready for an early night so I could be in top form the following day.

Samuel James Edward Fox

New School Day 2

This morning Dad decided he would drop me off. I was a little worried as I know he does not like being held up especially by traffic. Even though it is not the car in front that is at fault, he will sit on the horn and get angry. You just have to sit and be quiet knowing he will cool down soon.

We got into the car, and I remembered what Nan had said on her visit with me. Her words were work with mind messages and the law of attraction. What you want you need to think about ahead of the game then for sure what you want is what comes to you.

So, in I hopped and put on my seat belt. As I did, I thought to myself we are going to have the best easy ride to school. Then I remembered Nan said it is also important to say what you want out loud so, after thinking my thoughts to what I wanted, I then turned to Dad and said, "Dad, I reckon with that groovy shirt you have on today we are going to have all the cars get out of our way so we can get to school on time, and you can get to your meetings." He just looked at me with a smile and said, "Well son, that is great. Hey thanks for the compliment about my shirt. I do like this one. It always makes me feel on top of the world."

I leant back into the seat and relaxed. This way of working with words and positive thinking is going to get me through life.

Just as I had asked, the traffic was flowing and we got to the drop-off at school in perfect timing. Dad leant over and gave me a kiss on the cheek and said, "Have a great day. I will be picking you up this afternoon, so see you then." I said, "Thank you, I hope you have a great day too."

I watched him as he drove off then headed into school. I could not see Henry C or his friend. It was close to bell time, so I just headed into my classroom and found my seat. We had a stand-in teacher for the day who was rather nice. The morning went fast, and it was lunchtime before I even knew it.

As soon as the bell for lunch went, I headed outside to see if I could find Henry C and his friend. I could not remember her name. Sure enough, just as Henry C had said go to the tree at the back of the school, which is our HQ where we all meet each day, there was Henry C and this cute girl. Henry C introduced us both and we sat down to chat.

No sooner had we sat down when a bunch of bullies turned up. They started to pick on me and my weight. I just dropped my head in shame and started to fight back the tears. My mind went immediately to past events and school playgrounds where I was bullied and punched. Just when I thought I had a new life ahead of me I was back to the same story.

As I hung my head fighting back the tears, Henry C stood up and had a few major words to say to the bullies. In short, he told them if they kept going, he would be off to the Principal's Office to let her know what was going on. Just then Merthyr T stood up and said, "Mess with us and we speak up. You may remember those girls who were bullying me. Well we took it to the Principal. So, we can do it again if that is the way you are going to treat our friend."

WOW! There stood these two new friends of mine both standing up with powerful words to a group of bullies who didn't know what to say. All they did was turn and head off to find someone else they could bring down.

Henry C and Merthyr T gave me their hand and said, "Come on, stand up and stand tall, nobody messes with us."

I stood up and felt great. We all walked over to our special tree and sat down for lunch. I pulled out my lunch. Henry C had one look at it and said, "Are you serious man, do you know what all that carb processed food can do to your mind and body? Here, have one of my apples. So much better for you." I looked at him and at first felt down then I felt up. He was right. Mum just packs processed food full of sugar and carbs. It means she does not have to make me anything. There are always lollies and biscuits which she thinks are treats for me, but I guess they are actually wrong for me.

Henry C then turned to me after giving me an apple and said, "Mate can we have a serious talk? I don't want to hurt you, but we have to get real here. You are carrying a little extra weight, well more then you should be. It is not really healthy for you. Would you mind if I give you a bit of a hand and we take that body of yours and create a new one?"

I looked at him and I thought, mate I do hope you realise you are only 8yrs old. I know you have a head of red curly hair with those massive glasses that make you look like a professor, but how much do you actually know? Before I had a chance to think any further, Henry C started to talk again.

"Ok, let us put a plan into place. What you eat is what you end up looking like. When you move the body, you move the weight, and you move the mind. I reckon if we change what you eat, and we move the body we can use up the calories that you eat, and it won't take long, and you will have a new body. What do you say?" stated Henry C.

Right. Here is the plan SJ. We won't interfere with your Mums lunch boxes, we will let her come to conclusions in her own way. I think once she sees you changing, she will change. That is normally what happens with adults. Often, they can't get out of their own way until someone else around them makes changes then they make changes.

Just bring your lunch as you would normally and what we will do is spread the word that if anyone wants to swap an apple, banana or healthy meals for a chocolate, biscuit or unhealthy stuff you will swap. We will do it the right way and state that they can only swap a healthy lunch once a week. That way we will not be doing the wrong thing. What do you think?"

I thought. " Will this work? Henry C could see the look on my face and immediately made the statement, "This is going to work because we are going to make it work with structure, organisation and commitment." I was not going to argue with that.

Next Henry C said, "Diet is one thing, and we can surely work on your water intake to balance out the nutrition part, but you are going to have to exercise to use up the extra calories."

I agreed and said, "What about if at lunchtime I run around the oval a few times?" "Great idea, said Merthyr T. I can come with you, and I could do with a little extra fitness. What do you think Henry C?"

"Brilllant! You two but don't think I am running that oval; I do not need to lose any weight. But while you are both running the oval I will time you, as we want to improve the laps. Then once you have both run the oval let's play hand ball. We can do the special exercises that Chris Brazel teaches, which are awesome for the mind and the body. Do we all agree?"

"Yes" replied Merthyr T and SJ.

"Right, we start tomorrow. Bring your handballs and be ready as we are on a mission to create something awesome for all three of us." replied Henry C.

The bell then rang, and we all did a "take five" and headed back to class. The afternoon was awesome. The bully who came up to us outside was sitting in the back row. I just turned to him with a confident glare, and he looked away. Nobody was going to mess with me anymore.

I knew Dad was picking me up so as soon as I got out to the pick-up zone, I started to focus on what I wanted for our ride home. No busy traffic, clear lanes and a happy Mum when we walk through the door.

Dad pulled up and bent over to open the door. WOW he is changing. He asked how my day was and I said, "Great, how was yours?" He replied, "Great."

We then headed down the road to home. Sure enough the traffic was great, no idiots on the road. We opened the door and Mum was in a great mood again. This family was going to get on track.

Dinner was excellent until Mum said that she had bought a special cheesecake with cream for desert. I remembered what Henry C had said at school and said to Mum, "Do you mind if I don't have any. Your chicken and vegies were great and I really want to get fit and lose some weight, is that ok?" She looked at me with a grin and said, "Absolutely, I am proud of you." Dad then looked at me and said, "Son, that is impressive. I never thought I would hear you turn down chocolate cheesecake and cream. I am also impressed."

I just said, "Thanks". I then got up from the table and cleared the dishes into the dishwasher and headed to my room for homework and bed.

As I looked out my bedroom window, I saw a shooting star. Life was changing, I could do this. I could turn my life around. As I looked out of the window, Dad popped his head in to say good night and again he mentioned that he was proud of me for turning the chocolate cheesecake down. I simply said, "Thanks Dad, see you in the morning."

I finished off my homework and got into bed, my ears not hurting, my mind not racing, I felt cool, calm and at peace.

Now to keep this plan of my new body in action.

Samuel James Edward Fox

Action Plan for the New Body

It was lunchtime before I knew it. I grabbed my bag and headed to the tree. Just as I was getting close, this kid came up to me and said, "I believe you are SJ, and you are into trading lunches. How about I do Wednesdays? That is halfway through the week and by Wednesday I am over all the healthy food Mum packs? If you can put me down for Wednesdays, we have a deal, and I will meet you here and we can trade. I put out my hand and we shook on it. I no sooner started to walk to HQ when another kid came up to me with the same comment. He wanted Mondays as he felt healthy, fit food over a weekend was more then he needed and he wanted to kick off a week with something different. We shook on it and now Mondays was also booked.

Next minute Henry C turned up and asked how I was going. I said, "Great, can you believe these kids are coming up to me for trades on my lunches?"

"Of course I can. I have put the word out and the deal is we trade lunches. The rules are you can only trade on one day of the week. You can pull out at any time as it is a verbal agreement. The second rule is that to eat a sugar lunch you have to do one lap of the oval so the extra sugar is going to be run off and there will be no evidence.

"WOW! Henry C that is awesome. You are so clever."

"Yes, I am rather from time to time. I just love using my brain and doing negotiations. I believe there is always a solution if we just use our brain. We are actually getting the best of all worlds.

You get healthy lunches; they get to have a bit of sugar and you get to have company when you run around the oval. Everyone wins at the end of the day. I even get to win as I can show Chris Brazel my leadership skills, so I get to move into the next division. At the moment I am Level 1, but my aim is to be Level 8 by the end of the year. Now, are you ready to run? I have the stopwatch and we can time your first run of the oval. Merthyr T is away today so you will have to do it by yourself, but I have arranged for James to play the new handball game with you. He thinks he is a champion, so I told him you were also a champion and that he had better watch out. A bit of competition never hurt anyone."

"Right, Henry C, I better get on with the job. Here is my lunch. I am off around the oval before James turns up."

Off I went around the oval. Even though it was hard work carrying the weight I was carrying, I felt free, powerful and confident that I could do this. Henry C was now my coach as well as my best friend. My world was definitely changing.

I got back a little worn out. James had turned up ready for the handball. He pulled out a blue ball. I immediately thought blue ball, that connects to emotions. I just need to be smart about this. If he is using a blue ball, he is not confident. I reckon I can rock his boat before he starts.

I then bent over to my bag and pulled out my red ball and said, "How about we use a ball with power?" He didn't know what to say.

I started to bounce my ball as if I knew I was the champion. I did as Chris Brazel teaches you; left hand, right hand, left, right, left. James stood there totally uncertain about what was happening.

He agreed to play with the red ball. We kicked off and sure enough I had unsettled him. I only won by one point but winning by one point is a win.

We shook hands and congratulated each other. The bell went and we went back into school.

The afternoon went quickly, and it was time for pick up again. Mum was picking me up today as Dad was tied up in meetings until late.

We headed home and I got straight into schoolwork; I really wanted to keep on top of things in my life.

It was only Mum and I for dinner tonight which was nice as I got to chat to her. Normally Dad controls the conversation, and she just agrees.

I asked her about her day and how was work? She did look a little sad and worried. I noticed she had poured more than one glass of wine so I knew the day must not have been great.

We finished dinner and I walked over and gave her a hug and told her I loved her. She hugged me back and said, "I love you too."

I then headed to bed and had an awesome sleep.

Samuel James Edward Fox

Things Come Crashing Down

Morning came around so quickly; it was like I no sooner closed my eyes than it was time to get up and get going again.

We were running a little late and it was Dad's turn to drop me off. I quickly got into the car then realised I had forgotten my gym gear. Dad got really angry and started to yell at me about not taking responsibility for my life and my things. He then went on to tell me about all the time and effort he puts into work so I can have a great life.

I quickly got back into the car with my gym gear, put on my seat belt so we could head to school. We no sooner got down the road and a car pulled out in front of him. He immediately slammed his hand on the horn and went right off at the driver. This was not going to be a great trip to school.

Of course it was not his fault it was the driver's fault who pulled out doing the wrong thing. I just decided to be silent. That is the only way which works when he is in one of his moods.

We finally arrived at school. All he could say was, "Hurry up you are already making me late." I got out and headed into school. It was then I realised I had not worked on the mind message energies. I thought I better do that tomorrow.

Henry C was waiting at the gate so he must have sensed I had a problem. He was right there ready to give me the support and mind coaching I needed. I told him what had happened then he made me realise that it was not my problem. I had not caused the problem; it was an anger issue that my Dad had to deal with. He told me the best way is to send him love, not to get mad myself, just send my Dad love and mind messages that things will be ok.

Henry C had great news that we now had all the lunch deals we needed. He had mentioned that James was back for another round and put in the rule that today it was his blue ball. Henry C said that he had agreed provided James did a lap of the oval with me to make sure we had used up the same amount of energy. Then Henry C said, "As you go around the oval, each time you put your foot to the ground tell your mind that you are winning today with the blue ball." Man, this Henry C knows his stuff, no wonder he is a team leader in the Chris Brazel club.

Today I had 5 people including Merthyr T running the oval; it felt powerful. Of course, Henry C was on the sideline timing our laps. We finished the laps and James and I headed for our match. I had my mind totally prepared to win with the blue ball. I knew that if he needed to work with the blue ball, he was already worried and tied up in an emotion.

We kicked off and sure enough I won the first couple of points. At 5-2 to me I knew I had the game so then powered ahead and won 21-15. I was on a roll.

James congratulated me and we headed back into class. As we were walking back, James said, "SJ you are amazing, can you please teach me some of those moves you do before we play? It is like you connect to the ball so when you get into the game the ball just does what you want. I would love to learn that strategy if you can teach me."

WOW! Had I found my place in the world! I turned to him and said, "I would love to, they are simply MINDFIT Powerball exercises that Chris Brazel teaches you. It is amazing how you feel once you get into it. The colour of the ball is so important. If I were you, I would change the colour of your ball to red. Red is about confidence, power and focus."

James turned to me and put out his hand and said, "SJ you are a real man in this world today. I take my hat off to you. See you tomorrow, I will run the oval with you then we can practise."

"Super" I said, then back into school.

Dad was late in picking me up. I could tell before I even got into the car the ride home was not going to be great. I just got in and immediately said, "Thanks Dad for picking me up." He just grumbled back then his phone rang so he answered the call. The call did not go well. I could feel the anger boiling up inside of him.

We arrived home and as soon as I walked into the kitchen, I thought tonight is not going to be great. Mum had made a huge mess in the kitchen cooking jam. There were things everywhere.

Dad saw the mess then went right off his head about how hard he had worked all day and to come home to a mess like this was the last thing he needed. Mum didn't know what to say. I thought I could either stay or go to my room. I decided to go to my room. From my room I could head loud voices screaming and doors being slammed. The next minute I heard the car take off; it was Dad heading down the driveway.

I went out to the kitchen and saw Mum sitting on a chair with her head down and crying. I put my arm around her and said, "It will be ok, you sit there, and I will clean up the things."

It didn't take long, I had the dish washer full, and all the benches wiped down. As I did this Dad walked through the door and apologised to Mum. He then went on with this story about his day. They both had a hug and things were back to normal. Or should I say, Dad had his blow up, Mum did her crying, there were hugs and back to square one.

I went to bed, but before I turned in, I turned my selenite lamp on beside where I had a picture of Mum and Dad. Nan taught me that selenite lamps are great for cleansing energy in a room. I was going to cleanse the energy of my Mum and Dad.

What a day. Great day at school where I am making progress in amazing ways, but home is still the same with blow ups, arguments, crying and blame.

Morning came, and as soon as I woke up, I said thank you for the day, as Henry C had taught me. I also asked for the day, I wanted to come to me. Today was going to be totally different.

It was Dad's turn again to drive me to school. This time I remembered my mind messages for a positive drive to school.

I was definitely going to be on time so not to annoy him, take responsibility for my bags and what I needed for school. I was ready for the drive.

What did I get? Exactly what I asked and planned for. Thanks, universe, for helping me out.

Samuel James Edward Fox

The Championships

I was now two months at my new school. I had totally started to shape up. Even Mum and Dad were seeing the new me. I had to buy new clothes as the old ones did not fit.

My handball co-ordination was amazing. The other kids were actually joining me at lunchtime to learn new ways to work and train their brain.

We all did our oval runs together then into the ball exercises. We had our own amazing group. I would teach them about the colours and the different ways to work with the ball. It was like I had become the brain trainer. Henry C of course was still in charge and the top gun, but we all had a place, and we were creating something special in our group. Sure, Mum and Dad were still having their ups and downs and I never knew what the day was going to bring, but I was not getting as many ear twists or head slaps so that was a huge move forward.

Then the day came and our sports teacher walks up to our group and asked what was going on. We told him about the way we work on the oval then with our balls to train our brains to be powerful. I told him about the Chris Brazel's creative brain training system using the ball, colour and MINDFIT Power. He was totally taken with everything I said and asked how he could get in touch with Chris Brazel and learn more. He could see how this could benefit the whole school. I gave him Nan's number and said she knew Chris Brazel and would help him make contact.

I then said that the Annual Championships were coming up and I was going to compete along with the other kids that were training. He asked about the championships and said that he might like to take part as well. I explained that the way the championships work is that it is not all about you it is about working as a team.

To win the major event you had to compete in the single events then you had to have a family member compete with you, you also had to be able to outlast the wall using the left, right, left-brain work.

He stood there and said, "WOW that is actually so scientific and super amazing. I am definitely going to check out this lady and her work. I saw you when you first arrived, your head was down and I do believe you were a lot heavier then. If I am not wrong you had been expelled from 5 schools before coming here, is that right?"

I looked him right in the eye and said, "Yes, sir that was the old me, but I learnt my brain codes through Chris Brazel. I know me so I can be me. I don't have to be anyone else in the world just who I was born to be. I met Henry C when I first arrived and truly you should be congratulating him as it was he who has coached me to where I am today."

The teacher held out his hand and said, "Congratulations, I am so glad I am in your world and a teacher at your school. I will be in touch with Chris Brazel asap as this is what we need. No more talking about our problems, we need action and it sounds like this lady knows what she is doing." I said, "Great."

Just then Henry C turned up and I told him. He was so excited we had a game plan to go even further with our group and our way to help kids. Henry C was super excited as he could see now how easy he was going to be moving to Level 8 and head man for the club. Everyone was winning.

We checked out the dates for the championships we had 4 weeks to be fit, confident and on track with the training. We had 10 kids ready to all nominate for the championships. Chris Brazel was super excited to hear about our journey and invited us to a special training session. She is awesome. You just feel so amazing when you are working with her.

Now everything was on target except for one thing. To win the major event I needed a parent or grandparent to be in one of the sections. Sure enough I could win the individual events as well as the wall events, but I wanted to take out the whole championships and to do that I needed to ask Dad to join me.

I chatted about it with Henry C and as Henry C said, "Your Dad can either say, yes or no. You have nothing to lose and everything to win. Just as the ball has changed your life, you may be able to change your Dads' mind while training." I agreed.

I waited until dinner to check to see how his day had been. Luckily, he had had a great day. Mum was happy and they were both in a good mood so nothing like the present to pop the question.

I turned to him and said, "Dad, not sure if you know or not but I am top of the handball players at school. I even have a group I train under me. There is a major championship coming up and to win the majors I need a family member to be part of the team. Would you like to be my partner?" I had asked just as Henry C said. Ask for what you want; if you never ask you never know. I waited anxiously for his reply.

There was silence, even Mum was waiting uncertainly on how Dad would react. Then came the answer. "WOW! Samuel James that would be great. Did you know I used to play handball at school and I loved it and, believe it or not I too was a champion. Let's do this."

Game on. I had my Dad on my side. Next, I had to explain to him the rules and then the fact that we needed to practise. To my surprise he immediately agreed that to win you need to practise and put the effort in. Champions are people who focus with a goal and follow through to the end.

I gave him the dates and he agreed to be home early from the office, and we would work on the game. I told him about Chris Brazel and how we work with colours and the different exercises to train the brain from left, right, left, right etc. He said he would look up her work and get into it.

I must say that night I went to bed the most excited boy on the planet.

Over the four weeks Dad and I practised and practised even Mum would come out to the back yard and join in. It was amazing to see the whole family start to laugh as we played. In four weeks, there were no arguments. Dad was cooler as he drove me to school. Mum had decided that she didn't need wine each night which made Dad happy. She also started to make me healthy lunches, so all my school lunch deals had to fade away. The kids were not worried as they had joined in the handball games at lunchtime, so we were all on a mission to be powerful.

The day before the championships Dad came home super excited. He had been given a new head position. He was now in charge of the whole company; he was running the show. As we sat and talked over dinner which was now the norm, he told Mum and I how working with the ball each day he could focus so much more. He had got into the habit of taking his ball to work and when on the phone if he was having a hard time, he would bounce his ball against the wall. He said he could not believe how a simple exercise of working the hands, mind and feet with the ball made a difference in his mind, work and life.

The big day. We were ready. Mum came along as our supporter. She was no longer dressed in her blacks and greys, she looked awesome in this bright fuchsia pink with gold trimmings. Dad and I warmed up and we were ready. Bring on our competition.

Round one for both of us. We won. Round two for me. I won. Round three for Dad. He won. Round four both again. We won. Then the finals. Can you believe who we were up against in the finals. None other than my super sports teacher from school and his son. We rolled up our sleeves and on with the game. It was tight. We got towards the end; the score was level. One good hit and we would win. It was Dad's time to serve. He looked at me and for that one split second I could see a slight tear in his eye. A tear of pure joy and excitement, then there was a wink, and I knew game was on and we were going to win. It was like he opened his heart, soul and power all at the same time.

Yes, we did it. We won the super championships. It felt amazing. Mum was jumping up and down for joy and we were all hugging with excitement. The kids from school were super proud. Even Nan was there to congratulate me. I raced over to her and gave her a hug and kiss on the cheek. "Nan this all started with you, my codes, my room, my quilt and your love."

As you always say, love conquers all. "For where there is a will there is always a way."

Samuel James Edward Fox

We Found a Way to Love and be Mates

A few weeks passed and everyone was so happy in the house. We were finally working together as a team. Even Mum had fewer girls' nights out on the town.

Every Saturday we would pick a movie, and all sit down and watch it. We would take turns in who picked the movie. Dad loved his new CEO position. He was proud of the position he held and the goals he was kicking with his work.

I loved my new school; I was now a team leader with the lunchtime handball games helping the kids connect to the ball. Henry C was now being regarded as the Professor you go to when you need a change in your life. Merthyr T was right into her designer clothes and the kids were even starting to order t-shirts and jumpers directly from her and her Mum.

Who would have thought that your whole life can turn around so easily simply by working with your mind, your room, the words you use every day plus the simple way of working with the ball, colour and special exercises.

The best thing about all of this is my family changing at the same time. As Nan always says when you have love, things can fall into place. When you have anger, you create problems. The great thing was teaching Dad about the ball and the special exercises. It helped his mind just as much as mine. Even better still it was awesome when he listened to his Mum, my Nan. When he could see the changes in me, he knew that she had something to do with it. That is why he got his codes and Mum's codes done so we all got to understand each other. The best part of this journey is when I got to meet Chris Brazel when she came over and helped us with the energy of our whole home.

So amazing when she walked you through each room and showed you the MIND messages that you are creating. It was no wonder we were all sad, fighting and angry at each other.

Mum loved it when she found out why she would get bouts of depression and how to work with creativity to help her find her happy place. Now she paints amazing canvases and can you believe she is even selling them. She is creating a little business on the side.

Dad learnt that he has an anger energy that connects to past events and that he has to let them go. It was then he realised why the ball bouncing worked for him, as the ball connected to the floor or ground so he was able to release his anger and emotions with the special exercise movements and words.

The best part of all this journey was when Dad arrived home one day with a set of golf clubs specially made for me. The golf bag was this awesome red and white leather. It looked amazing. When I took out the clubs, they were the perfect fit. Dad even got a special cap in Navy with my initials on it. You see it was my 13th birthday. I said I didn't want a party I just wanted to have special time with him and Mum.

Apparently, he had seen a picture that I had placed on my vision board of Tiger Woods and the words I had written, I am going to be a top golfer like you. Dad loved his golf; he was only an average player but a super coach. That afternoon we headed to the golf course for our first hit. The best thing of all was that, instead of Dad just heading out to golf, Mum asked if she could come along and be my caddy. We were a family. We had found the pathway to the common dominator that pulls a family together which were two things a coloured bouncy ball and love.

My first lesson went great. Dad was so impressed that he signed me up as a member. He gave me the choice of professional lessons or lessons from him. I said I would prefer if he coached me as it would be our special time together. He agreed, so the next stage of my journey in life had begun. I was on the way to being a Pro Golfer with my Dad as my coach and my Mum as my caddy.

Never give up on life no matter how hard life feels today, or how sad you feel, or even if you are getting your ears pulled. If you seek the solutions and answers they will come. What you focus on is what you attract to you. Even though it may be hard to see the wood for the trees today just know that the sun comes up every single morning so every single day there is the opportunity to start a new way to life.

If you can, come and join the CB Club as it will be awesome. Henry C, Merthyr T, James and I are always there to welcome new members. We even have the "Know it all King" meet us on a regular basis teaching you about his experiences in life.

Catch you soon either in the CB Club or maybe we will meet at a handball championship or on the golf course.

Samuel James Edward Fox

Notes

A message direct from Chris Brazel

Thank you for being part of my world.

Always remember where there is a will there is always a way.

If we speak positive words our minds move into feeling so much better.

If we wear colourful clothes, we feel so much happier each day.

Come and join my club. It is fun and I would love for you to come along. You can even bring your dog along if you like.

Chris Brazel

Chris Brazel Products

Check out our website for
artwork, t-shirts, other books.

Join our club or come
join a boot camp.

www.chrisbrazel.com.au

www.ingramcontent.com/pod-product-compliance
Lightning Source LLC
Chambersburg PA
CBHW042052290426
44110CB00001B/32